An Eye
on Israel

Hans Bouma

An Eye on Israel

photography by **W. P. Weijland**
translation by **Sietze Buning**

William B. Eerdmans Publishing Company

With thanks to Jan van Heesen for advice and comment.

H. B.

With thanks to John Hanenburg for advice and comment on the translation.

S. B.

Copyright © 1978 by Wm. B. Eerdmans Publishing Co.
255 Jefferson Ave., S.E., Grand Rapids, Mich. 49503

This book is a translation from the Dutch edition (1976) of *Met Het Oog Op Israël*, published by Uitgeversmaatschappij J. H. Kok N. V. Kampen, The Netherlands. It appears by permission of Kok.

Library of Congress Cataloging in Publication Data

Bouma, Hans.
    An eye on Israel.

    Translation of Met het oog op Israël.
    1. Israel — Poetry. 2. Poetry of places — Israel.
3. Israel — Description and travel — Views. I. Weijland,
W. P. II. Title.
PT5881.12.09M4613   839.3'1'164   77-10641
ISBN 0-8028-1719-X

Introduction

You must not expect too much from this book — at least not from the text. You will not get from me a fully developed argument about Israel, no unique point of view on Israel, no theology of Israel. Moreover, I would not know how to help you acquire a consistent interpretation of Israel. Is not this land, this people far too mysterious and complex to be encompassed in one argument, one point of view, or one theology?

During my travels through Israel I simply took some rambling notes. Now that I look at them again, I recognize these fantasies as somewhat poetic. And they all have this in common: my own direct concern for Israel. This land, this people touches me deeply and personally. Israel reminds me of something, it challenges me, it poses questions for me, it baffles me, it amazes me: it always makes me think.

Gradually it becomes clear for me: what I write about Israel, I write about myself. Hence the title of the book. With an eye on Israel I discover who I am.

I hope that this book may also help you discover who you are.

HANS BOUMA

like a psalm
Mount Tabor resounds
upward from the plain

as high as heaven
it exalts
the Holy One

some hill
for a throne

nowhere else
does the earth sing like this

out of the very ground
of her being

nowhere else
does the view

extend so far
or offer so much

TABOR — Mount Tabor rises majestically in
the Valley of Jezreel. In Psalm 89 we read:
"Tabor and Hermon echo thy name." Ac-
cording to tradition, the Transfiguration
(Matthew 17) took place on this mountain.

he grew up
blossomed
and lived:
here

he lived
amid this fragrance
and color

a whole spring
a whole matchless spring
long

then the wind came
it snapped him
it jerked him away

flower of the field
lily anemone
the unforgettable

son of man

NAZARETH — In the spring the flowers shimmer on the hills of Nazareth —
the town where Jesus grew up. The fiery red anemones are especially
striking. Often the flower season is very short: "He blossoms like the flowers
of the field: a wind passes over them, and they cease to be, and their place
knows them no more" (Psalm 103).

you shall be born
in Bethlehem
that house of bread

you yourself are bread
you share yourself
you offer yourself

to the very last
until you die for it
you do God's will

that is, Jesus does

BETHLEHEM — In this "city of David" (literally, "house of bread") Jesus was born, who later would call himself "the bread of life." In front of Bethlehem broad terraces extend; all kinds of farming go on there. On the other side are the fields of Ephrata. At one time Bethlehem had abundant grain fields (Ruth 2).

on Mount Shemer
there you're sitting pretty
thought King Omri

safe
from God and enemies
summit of power

and he bought the mountain
and built his city:
Samaria

a proud fortress
invincible
who will hurt you —

but O
do the children realize anything

about the injustice
that reigned supreme
the humiliation of the poor

their time is now
and they need to hurry
with their goats

SAMARIA — King Omri founded a city here on Mount Samaria, which he bought from Shemer (I Kings 16:24). Surrounded by deep valleys, the city is strategically located. The prophetic criticism of Samaria is harsh: "You who persecute the guiltless, hold men to ransom, and thrust the destitute out of court" (Amos 5:12).

whatever
was ruined here

the faith
of Cornelius

still stands tall
and vigorous

just like the vision
of Peter

the witness
of Paul

the sermons
of Origen

and the hymns
of the nameless

everywhere
the stones
speak

CAESAREA — In 22 BC Herod began to build a typically Roman world capital in little, unimportant Caesarea. In AD 640 the Arabs conquered the city, and in 1107 the Crusaders. The latter built a mighty fort. In Caesarea Peter met the Roman centurion Cornelius (Acts 10); here Paul appeared before Agrippa (Acts 26). In the third century Origen lived here, renowned for his sermons. In the fourth century the famous Eusebius was bishop of Caesarea.

irresistibly
they opened for each other

that boy and that girl
in the shadow of the tree

aroused
they told their love

and no wonder
what else can they do

with the earth
opening up so amply

it pulls them along
demands a response

hearts are on tongues
mouths spill over
in blossoms and fruit —

land of loveliness
earth at its best

brimming health

ORANGE TREE — Here, for example, the lovers from the "Song of Songs" could have sat. "To sit in its shadow was my delight, and its fruit was sweet to my taste" (Song of Songs 2:3).

in their armor
with their legs crossed

they shine on their graves
in the churches of Europe

didn't they fight
the good fight?

these heroic knights
respected nothing

like holy places
conquered from Moslems

the military strategists
from out of their forts
ruled the whole district —

what they won
they lost

their fortresses ruins
their faith was powerless

in spite of all that, now
holy places are
holy

BELVOIR — This fort dates from the time of the Crusades (1099-1291). In 1168 the Hospitallers began its construction. Situated on a mountain south of the Sea of Galilee, this fortress commands a view of the entire Jordan Valley.

so this is it
city of my dreams
city of peace

forget it

city of discord
city of injustice
city of violence

at any moment
anywhere here
a bomb may explode

city of glamor
city of kitsch
city of commercialization

people try to make money
out of anything, even
out of the holiest

but I will not give up
I dream my dream
furiously

Jerusalem
shall believe in it

JERUSALEM — Panorama from the Mount of Olives. The Dome of the Rock is visible on the temple grounds. The ascending road leads to the Gate of Stephen.

the trees are still
shivering
the earth trembling

unforgettable
all those children
thrown

as sacrifices
to Moloch

to the murderous
hell of flames

"valley of murder"
Jeremiah cursed

"valley of hell"
people called it

I need to get away

shivering
shuddering
I go back

leaving the trees
and the earth behind me
in a deathly quiet

JERUSALEM — Valley of Ben-hinnom. In this valley children were offered
to Moloch. Jeremiah called this valley the "valley of slaughter" (Jeremiah
7:32). Before Jewish times this valley was called "ge-hinnom" (gehenna),
that is "valley of hell" (see for example Matthew 5:22). The "potters' field"
is also supposed to be found here, bought for thirty pieces of silver by Judas.

what it is
to be a sheep

to be
bargained for

to be sold
and betrayed

and afterwards
to be sent off
for slaughter

the man
from Nazareth

who called himself
shepherd
the good shepherd

he knew all about it

JERUSALEM — Every week the sheep market is held here at the wall. This spot remains unchanged by the course of time. Amos, the sheep raiser from Tekoa, must have come here with his animals.

fascinating
of course

all those caves
with traces
of habitation
as far back as the mid-
Paleolithic age

and you think about
that test of strength
between Elijah
and the priests of Baal

but

that lover
from the "Song of Songs"
how he must have loved
his lady beyond all
reasonable bounds

when he sang
"you carry your head
like Mount Carmel"

has ever man
exalted woman
in such splendor?

CARMEL — "Area of fruit"; "orchard." This ridge is about 20 kilometers long and 552 meters high; it forms the southern boundary of Asher. South of Haifa the ridge ends in a mountain cap in the sea. (For the hymn, see Song of Songs 7:5.)

so there he stands
a shepherd

(if you make some small talk
he'll pose for you)

but who is he really?

only
the flock he herds
knows

only
the ground he walks
knows

only
the roof of heaven
over his head
knows

CARMEL — A shepherd and his flock.

if the children
had not been there

the whole story
of the guide

would have left me cold

ACRE — Harbor north of Haifa. It was a Persian stronghold, a Roman colony, and the capital of the Second Crusaders' empire. In 1921 Acre was demolished by the Mamelukes. In the sixteenth century the Druse emir Fakhr-el-din built up the city once more.

what inspired them
those Jews

that they
conquered Masada

for three years
after the fall of Jerusalem
they offered resistance here
to the Roman siege

and finally
when they couldn't hold it
what inspired them
to throw themselves to death
collectively

(all but two women
and five children
who had hidden
in the aqueduct)

what inspired
those Jews?

what still always inspires them

MASADA — Out of this Jewish fortification, high and inaccessible on a mountainous pyramid on the west coast of the Dead Sea, Herod the Great made a genuine castle in 20 BC. Later Masada became a Roman garrison, which was conquered in AD 66 by Zealots.

you'd like to meet
the people

who
four thousand years ago
brought their offerings here

it would all be
so much clearer

yet

would they really
have much more to tell
than all these stones?

MEGIDDO — A Canaanite and Israelite city
lying at the exit of the Megiddo Pass between
the coastal plains and the Valley of Jezreel.
By about 4000 BC people already lived here.
Through excavations archaeologists have
found ruins of Canaanite temples from the
nineteenth century BC, a gate and stalls from
the tenth century BC, and an aqueduct from
the twelfth century BC.

springing alive
the water appears
out of the hillside

abundantly
it pours itself out
into the stream

and flows away
who knows
where?

Jeremiah
knew what he said

when he spoke
about God

as the fountain
of living water

AT DAVID'S SPRING — One of Israel's most plentiful springs, at the foot of Mount Gilboa. In Jeremiah 2:13 we read, "They have forsaken me, a spring of living water, and they have hewn out for themselves cisterns, cracked cisterns that can hold no water."

inside these walls
you're perfectly safe
if you're a sheep

at least
if you have a shepherd
who will be your door

a shepherd
like Jesus
for example

SINAI — Jesus alludes to such a sheepfold when he refers to himself as "the door of the sheep" and "the good shepherd" in John 10.

he lived here
he taught here
he healed the sick here

maybe
on this very place

he called himself
"the bread of life"

but stone
remains stone
and Jesus dead

unless
from the start

I take him
at his word
in faith

CAPERNAUM — Once grown, Jesus went to live in Capernaum (Matthew 4:13). The synagogue which Jesus regularly attended probably stood at this place, although these ruins are those of a synagogue of the third century.

here
for forty days and forty nights
the son of man breathed
the will of his Father

he saw visions
of peace and joy
and an earth where love dwells

his God could count on him
whatever it would cost him
even if it would cost his life

until the very end
he wanted to fulfill that will
of his Father
no power could stand in his way

THE WILDERNESS OF JUDEA — Into this barren, inhospitable region,
Jesus retired for forty days and forty nights after his baptism (Matthew
4:1-11).

no matter how much a stranger I am here —
tourist, outsider —

now and then an animal
even if it's only a goat

(usually
I can't stand goats
they eat my trees)

makes me feel easy again
I am recognized

I know my name again
for a moment I even feel

almost at home

PLAIN OF SHARON — This goat does what all goats like to do — stuff himself with twigs.

all my hopes
are revived again

peering across the hills
I see heaven on earth
it is irresistible

the wolf and lamb
shall graze together

the lion
shall eat straw like an ox

no death anymore
no sorrow
no complaint anymore
no trouble

God living with people
God all in all

whatever has happened
whatever will happen
in this land

what I see here puts me in tune
with the high pitch
of hope

NEAR JERUSALEM — Prophecies from Isaiah 65:25 and Revelation 2:3-4
work their way into the text.

I wanted so to call after him
but he was on his way already
lost in the crowd

that man from Nazareth

JERUSALEM — The old city.

endlessly
people mourn
declare their need here

no temple
no roof
over their heads

they pray and
they pray
up against these cliffs

they believe
they hope
they dream

the wall
sweats of it
the air is heavy

(and we
all the while
are taking pictures)

JERUSALEM — At the Wailing Wall (or
Western Wall), a part of the wall around the
temple of Herod, Jews have for centuries
mourned the destruction of their temple.

history lies buried here
twenty levels deep

in bits and pieces
it is all systematically laid out
in the Rockefeller Museum
in Jerusalem

but who were they
the people who lived here
what motivated them
what did they live for
what did they die for

for example who were
the eight-thousand spectators
who could occupy the theater
what moved them
what got them excited?

we know so little
I know only that Saul
and his son Jonathan

once upon a time, here
in Beth-shan
were dangling pitifully
from the wall

BETH–SHAN — Originally a Canaanite
stronghold in the Harod Valley, close to the
Jordan River. In excavations, layer upon
layer of civilization has been discovered both
from the bronze age and from the stone age.
In Beth-shan an almost perfectly preserved
Roman theater can be seen. For the heart-
rending story of the end of Saul and his sons
at the wall of Beth-shan, see I Samuel 31.

how the Holy One
got a foothold here

how salvation
sank its roots down here

how he
the son of man
went his way here

the yellow field cress
has understood it

(in contrast to
the crumbled wall
of defense)

BELVOIR — A view behind the gate of the old castle of the Crusaders at
Belvoir (twelfth century). In the valley below the Jordan flows. In the
background looms the Plateau of Gilead.

a cramp
pulled through the earth

shuddering
it cracked open

swallowed
Sodom up

and was still
still as death

it is
unbearable

you want to
cry out

want to swear
want to sing

but no sound
comes to your lips

Sodom —
a nightmare

a hell

SODOM — The catastrophe described in Genesis 19:25 (an earthquake in which the earth's crust sank away) occurred in the hilly terrain south of the Dead Sea during the middle of the bronze age.

they still are visible as ever
they stand tall, redreaming the dream

the mountains
are silent witnesses

of the name
He named

of the words
He spoke

expecting much
they look down on you

if only
for the sake of the mountains

you'd want to take with you
that name

and obey those words
no more, no less

SINAI — Mount Sinai (or Horeb), in the south of the Sinai Peninsula, is in the Bible the mountain of the covenant.

worth taking
a picture of?

sure

(and surely not
because Elijah fell down breathless
under such a bush)

but

where does such a
bramblebush get

in the forsakenness
of the desert

the courage
the spirit
the persistence

to be
so invincibly
so broad-branchedly
so thrivingly and completely

a bramblebush?

BRAMBLEBUSH — Here and there you see this bush in the wilderness.

so purposeful
as he plows
through the earth

panting
sweating
for the sake of his family

not looking back
but being alert

(stones everywhere
roots like branches)

he hopes
for fruitfulness

he dreams
of a good harvest —

fit for the
Kingdom of God

A PLOWER — As in Luke 9:62: "No one who sets his hand to the plough and then keeps looking back is fit for the Kingdom of God."

after the kitsch
of the Church of the Nativity —

where it's likely
you'd lose your faith —

after the racket
of the market —

with its horrible
cooped-up, half-dazed
chickens and turkeys —

I landed finally
in this little street

and inhaled
for a minute

(but long enough)

the miracle

BETHLEHEM — In a building such as this Jesus could have been born.

suppose that thirty-five years ago
I had been born

not in Tilburg
but in Nablus

as son of a
Samaritan man and a
Samaritan woman

(and why not)

then every year
I would come
with a few hundred others

to this holy hill
to celebrate the Passover

full of devotion
we would kill twelve lambs
we would offer the intestines
we would eat the flesh

GERIZIM — On this hill (a little to the south
of Shechem) the blessing was to be said, ac-
cording to Deuteronomy 27:12. Mount
Gerizim is the holy mountain of the Samari-
tans. Each year the small Samaritan com-
munity of Nablus celebrates the Passover
here.

everything here
makes you think

sometimes makes you hope
sometimes makes you sing

sometimes makes you despair
sometimes makes you stop talking
and be very quiet

what do I look for here
God knows

in some way
here

I need to come
to terms with myself

get it together

JERUSALEM — Mt. Scopus at the east side of Jerusalem, one of the hills that circle the city.

that Absalom lies
buried here

in a grave, mind you,
from the first century
after Christ, why

nobody believes it

still
everybody speaks about
"Absalom's grave"

so do I

that way his name
still gets mentioned
a little

JERUSALEM — In the Valley of Kedron, on the eastern rise, are a few
graves hewn out of rock, dating from the time of the second temple. One is
called "Absalom's grave."

I still don't know
which tree
fascinates me more

the almond tree
which is the first
in full bloom
but the last
to yield fruit

or the mulberry tree
which is the last
to bloom
but the first
to display fruit

just as I still don't know
which kind of person
fascinates me more

ALMOND TREE — This tree, which originated in India and Persia, blooms already at the end of the winter, even before the leaves have sprouted. The fruit doesn't come until late summer.

leave your gods
at home

at least if you expect to
escape from here
all in one piece

in the grand manner
Elijah
bedevils them

do not play devil's advocate
for those powers
you so rely on

forget them
swear off allegiance to them
those ideals
to which you offer up everything

it's been demonstrated conclusively
that there's no point to it

CARMEL — At this place the contest occurred between Jahweh, the God of Israel, and Baal (I Kings 18). A modest sign is at the spot where the altar stood.

six tribes
on Mount Gerizim
to bless

six tribes
on Mount Ebal
to curse

and between them
a people

a people
on their way
of salvation
and damnation

a people
that will define
the course of history

you'd better belong
to this people

then for your whole life
you're marked

EBAL — On Mount Ebal (north of Shechem) the tribes of Reuben, Gad, Asher, Zebulun, Dan, and Naphtali had to gather together to pronounce the curse (Deuteronomy 27:13-26; Joshua 8:30-34).

ten-thousand years of history
and we covered them
in three hours

and we even took
a half-hour break
for lunch

JERICHO — One of the very oldest cities, situated in the Jordan Valley.

they thought the place holy
the Essenes

"chosen of the Lord"
they were

the end of the world
was coming soon

and they
"sons of light"

would conquer
"the sons of darkness"
once and for all

they are dead
and the world went on

but does that alter the case?

they thought the place holy
the Essenes

it is

QUMRAN — Ruin on a marl terrace about 800 meters from the northwest
coast of the Dead Sea. In the second century BC the sect of the Essenes
established themselves here. The Dead Sea Scrolls were found in grottos
around these ruins.

bending down thirsty
over the water

David saw
his own face

and knew afresh
who he was

ENGEDI — Pursued by Saul, David hid away in a cave near Engedi — an
oasis on the west coast of the Dead Sea (I Samuel 24). Although he had the
chance, he did not kill Saul.

you wonder about Israel

the certainty
with which God planted
his people in this land

the endless care
with which he surrounded them

but more
you wonder about yourself
and you ask amazed

why
doesn't he give up on us?

VINEYARD — The neglected state of affairs
in this vineyard reminds one of Isaiah 5:1-7.

why do I refuse
to tolerate
violence
in Israel

it is, after all
a people like any
other people

with manpower
and weaponpower
it struggles for its existence

all right

but no people has awakened
such expectations

still awakens such expectations
in me

MITLA PASS — Here, during the Six-Day War in June 1967, Israel won a victory over Egypt.

they wrote words
that people study with bated breath
more than two-thousand years later

but our words
are so fleeting
on our lips they die already

do we really live?

and still it was a hand
of a Nabataean
that wrote this

a hand like yours
a hand like mine

INSCRIPTION — This inscription is by the Nabataeans, a Semitic commu-
nity that came from the Arabian wilderness about four or five centuries BC.
They established themselves at the fringes of the more established cultures.
Later the Nabataeans established a vast empire that included the entire
region of Trans-Jordan.

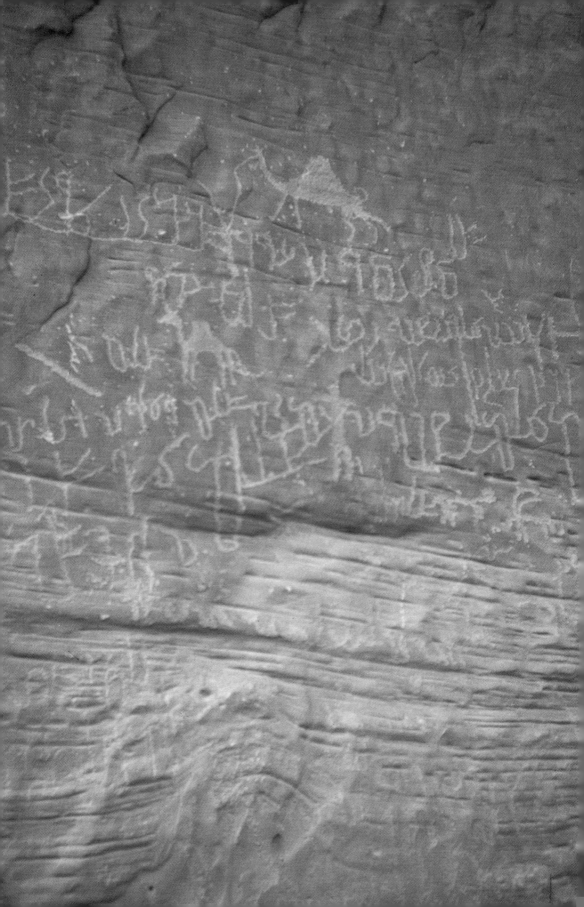

without there being
any good reason for it

a grace is granted

between the bare rocks
all at once a few flowers

indeed
miracles have not ceased
in the earth

WILDERNESS — Just a few flowers.

clearly
a city over which
a judgment has passed

Micah already saw
the storm lowering

"a heap of ruins in the
open country"
he prophesied
bare foundations

but hear Philip
proclaim
the Kingdom of God

and see the people
thronging about him
all ears

and see him baptize
nothing but baptize

Samaria

clearly
a city over which
last of all
grace has passed

SAMARIA — Remains of all kinds of proud architecture — Ahab's, for
example — strew the ground here. Philip's visit to Samaria is told in Acts
8:4-25. The prophecy of judgment is found in Micah 1:6.

retreat
clear your head
drop everything

and be silent be silent
alone with yourself
alone with your God

and listen
breathe deeply

forty days
forty nights long

and you will see
that it's true

the Kingdom of Heaven
is close to us

WILDERNESS OF JUDEA — In this desert
John the Baptist preached, "Repent; for the
Kingdom of Heaven is upon you" (Matthew
3:1-2). The wilderness functions repeatedly
in the Bible as a place for turning inward and
for experiencing Messianic visions.

how in his element
he was here
at the shore of the lake

talking preaching
healing liberating
distributing bread and fish

a brother
one of us
man among men
person among persons

it was the death of him
anybody who lives like that
needs to be eliminated

he came back
nobody recognized him
the risen one

he came back
at the shore of the lake
he's one of us for good

listen
his voice echoes
over the water

SEA OF GALILEE — In the days of Jesus the shore of this lake was much busier than it is now. Many, many people lived here, and there were markets, sheepfolds, synagogues, theaters, racetracks, etc. It was also called the Lake of Gennesareth and the Sea of Tiberias.

*he spoke here
in language unequalled*

*words of fire
words of bread*

*words that were to change
the world —*

*words that just lie there
for the gleaning*

*but look out
don't burn your fingers*

*whoever touches them
must do them*

MOUNTAIN OF THE BEATITUDES — On this mountain, actually only a hill, Jesus is thought to have spoken the beatitudes. It is in the vicinity of Capernaum.

everything is recorded on it
from Abraham
to the ghetto in Warsaw

and nearby
in the Knesset
people are discussing
what will happen to Israel
in the future

whatever happens
"neither through force of arms
nor by brute strength"
is what I read

it sounds beautiful
but what must they do with that
there in the Knesset —

what must I do with it?

JERUSALEM — In front of the Knesset (the parliament building) stands the
Menorah, a seven-branched candelabra. On the seven arms, twenty-nine
panels depict figures and events from Biblical and Jewish history. On the
two last arms we read: "Neither by force of arms nor by brute strength, but
by my spirit! says the Lord of Hosts" (Zechariah 4:6).

bending down
over their writings

I find the characters
gradually
begin to lead a life of their own

I discover
facial features

weather-beaten heads
of old monks

I see faces

faces
so strange
and so trusted

as only faces
can be

JERUSALEM — In this building ("The Shrine of the Book") are the Dead
Sea Scrolls, discovered in Qumran in 1947. Reminiscent of the jars in which
the scrolls were discovered, the roof has the form of the top part of a jar.

mid-March
and the Feast of Purim

fun and games
good excuse for a party
like Mardi Gras

meanwhile
the Book of Esther
hardly acquires historical
authenticity

but what does that matter?
whether it happened or not

a feeling of liberation
tingles in young and old

(and besides,
the story is so true
to the feeling, that it really
could have happened)

JERUSALEM — The Feast of Purim is a
celebration of the deliverance of the Jews
under Ahasuerus, as recorded in the Book of
Esther. The book of Esther intends to make
the Feast of Purim legitimate; originally it
had been a Persian feast.

you try to overlook it

and a visit like this
to Mount Carmel, for instance
is interesting and marvelously
diverting, but you can't escape it

here too nature is violated
here too they have bio-industry

(in an army artillery outpost
I saw women working
the old concentration camp
numbers on their arms:
certainly they know what's what!)

here too they have atomic energy
etcetera

it's enough to make you despair
when in Israel mind you —
where all creation ought to be safe —
they don't respect life anymore

where then?

CARMEL — The drinking basin indicates the place where Elijah ordered
the jugs to be filled with water three times, all to be poured over the altar
(I Kings 18:34-35).

just a detail
but something like this
preoccupies me for hours:

where would David get
the five smooth stones
now

to floor that violent giant
Goliath
with

now that the brook
that once was
is dried up?

TEREBINTH VALLEY — In this valley (also called the Valley of Oaks) the conflict between David and Goliath took place. At the very place where once the brook flowed, we find a pump and irrigation pipes.

everywhere it strikes you
this concern for water

people have devised
the most ingenious access-,
distribution-, and storage-systems

so that they wouldn't be caught
without water or with
polluted water

the Romans, for example,
built complete aqueducts
here

but the principle
that water
pure water
is priceless
and the basis for all
health and prosperity

we ourselves
will need to discover that
from scratch

CAESAREA — One of the aqueducts by which the Romans brought good drinking water from Mount Carmel to the city.

why should I need
so maddeningly much

why should he need
so maddeningly little

just to be able to live
to be able to be
a person on earth?

BEDOUINS

silos full of grain
reservoirs full of water
jugs full of oil

silos full of courage
reservoirs full of hope
jugs full of faith

silos full of corpses
reservoirs full of blood
jugs full of tears

MASADA — One of the grain silos in that fortress where fewer than a thousand Jewish rebels were able to withstand a Roman siege for three years (AD 70-73).

you are a stranger here
nothing can change that

even if you plant a tree
(and what better gesture here)

you will never be at home here

no more than that other stranger
Jesus of Nazareth

your brother

NAZARETH — One of the many places in Israel where reforestation is in progress. From outside of Israel you can make a modest contribution and have a tree planted here.

in a comfortable bus
with a capable driver
and a reliable guide
and perfect air-conditioning

we went into the wilderness

we found it
a long, tiresome journey

but naturally
what a wilderness is
you'll never learn this way

and even less
an oasis

EL ARISH — At this oasis the Sinai Wilderness begins.

a donkey
head-to-hoof humility
head-to-hoof grandeur

no matter how loaded down
with packs and sacks
no matter how whipped along

he keeps his dignity:
Messiah's chosen steed

uttermost humility
uttermost grandeur

JERUSALEM — The way to the Scopus. See
Zechariah 9:9 and Matthew 21:1-11.

more mysterious
more accessible

prouder
humbler

chaster
earthier

more regal
more human

this lady

JERUSALEM — You never see men with a jug or basket on their heads.

you go to Israel
you visit holy places

and what do you find?

the howmanyeth confirmation
(though a unique one)
of what you knew already:

that salvation is as earthy
as Israel is earthy

and that Jesus is your brother
just as every Jew is
your brother

SAMARIA

only one God

whose love
is unshakable

whose faithfulness
is solid as rock

whose mercy
is high as heaven

and he ratifies
his covenant
with his people

here

SINAI — Along this path you reach the top of the mountain.

of course you know him

the God of Abraham
Isaac and Jacob
the God of the covenant

for years you've lived with him

you've learned to trust him
you're able to dream his words
you know what he wants from you

but the view
here

the view
makes everything different

the view —
and the silence

SINAI — The top of the mountain. Monks have built a chapel here.

*everything here
is so fulfilled by him*

*that the little hills
whisper his name*

*that the wind
sings his words*

*that the water
cherishes his image*

*and so
if he walked here
we*

*could hardly
recognize
him*

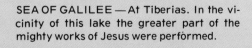

SEA OF GALILEE — At Tiberias. In the vicinity of this lake the greater part of the mighty works of Jesus were performed.

as in a vision
he saw
that he was right

that the way he went
was the only way

he stood there glorified —
Jerusalem Jerusalem

he stood there glorified —
death before his eyes

the Son, the beloved —
a person fulfilling the law
man after God's own heart

TABOR — On this hill Jesus is said to have been transfigured (Matthew 17:1-13). Important here is Matthew 16:21: "From that time Jesus made it clear to his disciples that he had to go to Jerusalem, and there to suffer much from the elders, chief priests, and doctors of the law; to be put to death. . . ."

so well-grounded
so steadfast

so far-reaching
so dependable

so generous
so full of blessing

so indestructible

no
my faith
will never be
that strong

OLIVE TREE — On the Mount of Olives.

where do you come from
what are you doing here

I asked the tree

where do you come from
what are you doing here

he replied

finally
after a long talk
we agreed completely

SINAI DESERT

so polluted
the water from
the River of Paradise?

it is not
the children's fault

and certainly not
the fault of that boy
and that girl

who walked slowly
along with the water
through the tunnel

so that gradually
they could find each other
for good

JERUSALEM — The Siloam Tunnel. King Hezekiah had a tunnel of 512
meters carved out of the slope of the temple mountain. It goes from the
Gihon fountain to the pool of Siloam (II Chronicles 32:30). In Ezekiel's vision
(47:1-12) the water from the temple mountain brings about the cir-
cumstances of Paradise. One of the rivers of Paradise was called Gihon
(Genesis 2:13).

is it after all only a dream?

swords
into plowshares

spears
into pruning hooks —

a dream?

everyone sitting
under his grape vine
under his fig tree

peace at last

anxiously
the fig tree
gropes for the future

craning its neck
with longing

the whole creation
waits

SAMARIA — In the foreground figtrees — with their big, finger-shaped leaves. The trees are referred to in Micah 4:1-5 and in Romans 8:19.

wherever I go

everywhere this question:
who is Israel?

everywhere this voice:
give this people a name

but I hesitate
then scribble back

my answer
has in it the name
I give this people

it reflects
who I am

it is my name

SINAI WILDERNESS — An oasis.

as though creation
were beginning again

light comes here
before daybreak

celebrating victory
promising everything

does God's face
dawn this way everywhere
on earth?

just so
God's face dawns

over Israel